Count It All Joy

JERRY LEWIS

ISBN 979-8-89345-425-3 (paperback)
ISBN 979-8-89345-426-0 (digital)

Christian Faith Publishing
832 Park Avenue
Meadville, PA 16335
www.christianfaithpublishing.com

Printed in the United States of America

To my wife, Kim,
my daughter, Savanna,
and my son-in-law, Josh,
along with our Freedom Christian Fellowship family

INTRODUCTION

I am passionate about being a pastor—it is my heart, my love, and my primary calling in life. My wife, Kim, and I have been pastors for around thirty-three years, with thirty of those years dedicated to serving the Freedom Christian Fellowship family. Being part of this community has been an incredible journey, and we love our Freedom family dearly.

In 1994, at the age of thirty-three, we became pastors of what was then known as East Pittsburg Pentecostal Church. Before this, I worked as a truck driver for Coyne Textile Services and served as an evangelist and associate pastor for about three years.

Our church started to grow, and in November 2001, we moved into a new, expansive facility that was twenty thousand square feet. Along with this growth came moments of awe-inspiring signs, wonders, and miracles; but we also faced significant challenges. I often say, "The bigger the lights, the bigger the bugs!" Growing pains are real, and as they say, "No pain, no gain!"

I am immensely grateful for the perseverance, power, and comfort found in the Word of God and the Holy Spirit. They have sustained us in our lowest points and most vulnerable moments.

I felt compelled, commissioned, and inspired by the Holy Spirit to write this book shortly after concluding a series at our church, "Count It All Joy," which is, of course, the title of this book. God desires His church, His body, His disciples, and His followers to walk in the fullness of His joy.

May this book inspire and encourage you to choose to walk in the absolute joy of the Lord.

Blessings,

Jerry Lewis

CHAPTER 1

Count It All Joy

I have faithfully served the Lord for over forty years. My radical salvation occurred in my 1974 burnt-orange four-cylinder Ford Pinto when I was about twenty. It may sound peculiar, but under intense conviction, the Holy Spirit was knocking at my heart. The night Jesus gloriously saved me, I was never the same again.

The happiness and joy that filled my heart were unexplainable—joy unspeakable and full of glory. Quoting John 15:11 (NLT), Jesus said, "I have told you these things so that you will be filled with my joy. Yes, your joy will overflow." On that glorious night, Jesus filled me to overflowing with His heavenly joy.

Consumed and changed, I desired everyone to experience this joy. I joined a local church, ready to do whatever was necessary. However, in my attempt to fit in and be accepted, I witnessed a side of church life I never knew existed, leading to a split over a trivial matter.

Subsequently, I joined another church, Seven Pines Pentecostal Church, where my wife and I officially became a couple, marrying on April 16, 1983. In 1987, my wife gave birth to our daughter Savanna, and that same year, I accepted my call into ministry. With a newborn and a new ministry, our family launched into evangelism. Lives were saved, people received the Holy Spirit, and I loved preaching.

After short stints of pastoring, I discovered that joy and religion don't always go hand in hand. The first place we pastored was Egypt Pentecostal Church in Jackson County, Kentucky. Not many ministers can say they pastored in Egypt. In 1994, after much prayer, we started pastoring where we are to this day, Freedom Christian Fellowship. At the time, it was known as East Pittsburg Pentecostal Church.

About a year and a half into our pastorship, the wind of the Holy Spirit began to blow. Seemingly every week, somebody was being saved and set free. It was like a spiritual bomb went off—enormous numbers of people were getting saved. Preaching was easy, and the anointing and power of the Lord were life-changing. Joy filled the house!

Soon, we were out of room. The pews were full. The parking lot was maxed out. We were setting out chairs in our sanctuary to seat the masses who were flocking to see how God was moving. However, at a time when the congregation was full of excitement and joy, religion—the enemy of joy—stuck up its ugly head and wanted full control.

As a young, hungry pastor struggling with what to do, I found myself depleted but not defeated. I wanted to handle the situation right, but I was dreading the inevitable confrontation. Persecution comes in various forms, and Psalm 34:18–20 (KJV) reassures us, "The LORD is near to the brokenhearted; He saves the contrite in spirit."

The word *afflictions* in verse 19 is plural, encompassing unkindness, evil, distress, misery, injury, calamity, and adversity. The only way to operate in true joy is when attacks are combated with the revelation of who we are in Him (2 Timothy 3:12 KJV). I have experienced that what the Lord doesn't deliver you from, He will deliver you through.

When attacks come from within, it cuts deeper and takes longer to heal. I had to learn to live according to James 1:2–3, "My brethren, count it all joy when ye fall into divers temptations; Knowing this, that the trying of your faith works patience." I had to live in joy despite man's accusations, to walk in joy despite critical statements about doing things differently than the religious norms.

When Jesus came, it was the most religious time known to man. He was considered uncouth by some because they thought he lacked sophistication. Some judged Him harshly because He did not act or react religiously or respond religiously like they anticipated Him to do. Instead, He restored humanity to a fresh covenant relationship with God the Father, contrary to the old covenant and filling its void, representing a covenant bringing healing, help, and hope.

If you spend your life pleasing man, you will never fulfill God's intended assignment. Don't waste time seeking the approval of people who frankly don't matter. That is not intended with any malice or viciousness, so please do not misunderstand. My question is, why do we seek the approval of man, when we should be seeking the affirmation of God? Seek affirmation from God.

More than man's confirmation, we must have God's affirmation. More than man's endorsement, we must have God's enforcement because what God starts, He finishes (Philippians 1:6). It is our job to compete, but his job to complete!

> *Compete.* "To strive to gain or win by defeating or establishing superiority."
> *Complete.* "To bring to a desired and victorious conclusion."

It's our job to compete, striving to gain or win. It is His job to complete, bringing it to a desired and victorious conclusion. Our joy cannot only be based on others' opinions. Our joy must be based on the revelation of who Jesus is in us (Matthew 5:11–12).

I have discovered that true joy takes discipline to both operate in and live in. To count it all joy means to be able to calculate, calibrate, and evaluate from a spiritual perspective and not from a natural or carnal perspective. The true joy of the Lord isn't man-focused or religion-based but Christ-centered! Joy is an outward expression of a genuine inward experience with the Lord Jesus, so real and life-changing that you know you will never be the same again.

Many think that achieving a certain status in life will flood them with happiness and joy. Yet that is a fake mirage and cheap imitation of true reality. Because you can have more degrees than a thermometer and accomplishments that may provide opportunities and resources, but they cannot bring the eternal, internal, and perpetual joy that is not influenced by seasons or emotions. These things may help you obtain the things you have never had in your past but longed for. It may even bring you some sense of accomplishment and, yes, even some form of happiness. It may even get you connected with the upper echelon of society. However, it will never be able to bring you the true joy of the Lord.

As born-again believers, we can count it all joy because our faith and confidence are in the Lord. We don't live according to the flesh but according to the spirit, changing everything when life's tests and stresses come our way, counting it all joy the entire time. When the stressors of life come our way, we can count it all joy. When things are not going the way we thought they would or intended for them to go, we can still count it all joy, because the joy of the Lord is our strength.

In a world deceived by polished politicians and religious alternatives that are deceiving and desensitizing the people making God whoever they want Him to be, the true church must love, lead, forgive, heal, teach, and disciple in the love and standard of the Lord Jesus. The mindset of many is that you deserve to be happy, so you do whatever it takes to accomplish that. This deceptive, demonic lie will damn many to the eternities of hell. But a true encounter with the Lord gives the sought-after peace and happiness. Psalm 144:15 (KJV) states, "Happy is that people, that is in such a case: yea, happy is that people whose God is the Lord."

Do you know the difference between happiness and joy? The difference is you can buy happiness but can't purchase joy. Joy is internal, eternal, and perpetual—not seasonal or superficial. New homes, new cars, new clothes, and new things do bring some form of happiness, but happiness is always affected and influenced by emotions. The difference between happiness and joy is that happiness is a natural expression, while joy is a supernatural way of life.

CHAPTER 2

Evaluation

Evaluate, by definition, means "to determine the value of something." It means to determine the significance, worth, or condition of something, usually by careful appraisal and study. When we properly evaluate things as born-again believers, it is a compliment to us because we have decided to make a real conscious godly decision and to not be too hasty in our decision.

Wisdom says to evaluate. Maturity says do not be so quick to conclude. Proper conclusions can come to pass when wisdom and maturity are involved. Because Scripture said that it is the patience—the enduring, sustaining perseverance—that we believers possess and maintain that keeps our souls (Luke 21:19). Evaluation reveals a seasoned level of understanding that has been gained through experience.

We must allow our life experiences to become life lessons to teach, help, and navigate other followers and disciples of Jesus. Sadly, many allow life's disappointments to cause them to become wounded, bitter, hardened, and even critical. When we choose after careful consideration and evaluation, we can convert the bitter to the better, because that is when an axe can be laid to the root of the problem that will bring release, relief, and restoration to the soul. Healing can only come when there is a revelation of what the Word says concerning the situation. And it is the revelation that has been obtained beforehand that can give you the right observation and consideration when struggles come or the battle intensifies and elevates.

Evaluation is the ability to learn to wait! Isaiah 40:31 (KJV) says, "But they that wait upon the LORD shall renew their strength; they shall mount up with wings as eagles; they shall run, and not be weary; and they shall walk, and not faint." Sadly, the problem is that many believers are not patient waiters! We want it fast, quick, and now! But why rush it and crush it? The ability to wait is the ability to prepare and be ready for when the right time for release comes. The word *wait* is not a passive or unaggressive word but is in fact a word of expectation and anticipation. The word *wait* really means that while you are showing maturity through evaluation, you are looking for your release at any time and at any moment according to the timing of the Lord. God's timing trumps our timing every time (Luke 14:28–30 KJV).

Evaluation allows things to be seen clearer, in more depth, and with more precision. Evaluation on a personal level reveals how we think, how we perceive, and how we truly view things from a spiritual perspective in the Lord. We all need a true evaluation of ourselves, not one that is not based upon religion, philosophy, or church doctrine. But it should be one based upon relationship and godly fellowship with the Holy Spirit.

Some of the most miserable and mean people I know are professing born-again believers. And I wholeheartedly believe that the reason many of them are the way they are is because they are spiritually miserable and do not possess the true joy of the Lord. If we allow man's philosophies, doctrines, and personal interpretation dominate and dictate us, we will never walk in the provision, the promise, or the power that the Lord Jesus intended for us to walk in individually as a person and corporately as the church.

Sadly today, things are either overspiritualized where there is a demon behind every door and under every rug, or there is a numb denial to even admit that there is any spiritual adversity or battles at all. The truth is, they are both wrong. Some may suggest that there is our natural walk in life, and then there is our spiritual walk in life. But truthfully as born-again believers, there are not two walks in life:

a natural one and a spiritual one. There is only one, and that is our personal spiritual walk with the Lord Jesus. Where we do not allow the flesh to usurp the spirit, but where we allow the spirit to usurp the flesh.

May I challenge you today to view it from a totally different perspective? Instead of us being the natural trying to navigate spiritual, let's be the spiritual navigating in the natural! What's the difference? The difference is *evaluation*. To *evaluate* means to determine the significance, worth, or condition of something usually by careful appraisal and study.

You were created on purpose, with purpose. Allow that to marinate in your mind a bit. The circumstance was not that you were born and then God tried to decide something for you to do. Rather, you were born because God had a need, and you were the one He created to fulfill that assignment. When a person becomes born again by confessing their sins and dedicating their lives to the Lord Jesus, their heart was saved, not their head. Allow me to say that again: your heart was saved, not your head. Please receive that in your spirit. Even though we are saved, we now must align the head with the heart, because the natural man wants to evaluate from a natural perspective, but the heart evaluates from a supernatural perspective.

Proverbs 23:7 declares that "as a man thinks in his heart, so is he." The word *think* here is a mathematical and intellectual term that means "to properly ponder, estimate, and evaluate the worth and importance of something"! *Heart* in this context is not necessarily referring to the natural heart such as a heartbeat, but rather the activity of the mind and the seat of one's emotions. Therefore, it is incredibly significant and of profound importance how we look, how we estimate, and how we view ourselves. This is where there must be a revelation of 2 Corinthians 5:17 (New International Version) Therefore, if anyone is in Christ, the new creation has come: The old has gone, the new is here.

Yes, there is an undeniable battle between our flesh and our spirit, but our battles should never be permitted or allowed to steal our joy, our confidence, and our assurance of who we are and whose we are in the kingdom of heaven. Born-again believers are new creations. A new creation is a creation that had never been before! Jesus has truly made all his followers brand-new.

In 2 Corinthians 10:3 (NKJV), Paul shares, "For though we walk in the flesh, we do not war according to the flesh." We have been called to be warriors, not worriers! Therefore, we cannot afford to allow the battles of life to dictate, dominate, or eclipse the purpose, the plan, and the agenda of the Holy Spirit for each one of us. All believers should remind themselves daily of 1 Corinthians 6:20 (KJV): "For ye are bought with a price: therefore, glorify God in your body, and in your spirit, which are God's." As believers, we belong to God, period. That settles it. No more questions to ask! And if God purchased us through the blood of His dear Son, that means that we can walk and live in his victory and his joy at the same time if we are following His word.

True joy releases a level of confidence that can transform the mundane into the miraculous. True joy doesn't exempt us from attack, but it allows us to face it with a level of confident assurance that brings overcoming and prevailing victory. Joy has layers to it. With each revealed layer comes a new revelation of something greater and more powerful. Joy is much like salvation in that it doesn't just occur once, but it is perpetual and continual in its evolution and progression.

Joy not only brings strength and confidence in our lives, but joy glorifies the Father. Isaiah 43:7 declares that we were created for His glory! Glorifying God with our bodies comes through the evaluation of who the Word says that we are in Him and not who the world says we are. There is great joy when we know who we are in the Lord.

> *2 Corinthians 5:17.* We are a new creation.
> *2 Corinthians 5:21.* We are the righteousness of God.
> *Ephesians 1:5.* We have been spiritually adopted.
> *Colossians 2:10.* We are whole and complete in Him.
> *Jeremiah 29:11.* He has plans for us.
> *Isaiah 53:5.* We are healed.

The list of scripture goes on of who He says that we are in Him and what He has given us access to. But until we have our own personal revelation of who we are in Him, we will continue to live beneath our privilege of being truly free, liberated, blessed, and walking in the true joy of the Lord.

Joy is systematic more than it is automatic. *Systematic* means that it is "done according to a fixed plan or system." Joy is methodical, which means that it is done "according to an established form of procedure." Joy is not limited to an outward expression, but it is also the revelation of an inward possession. In fact, the outward expression displayed is the direct result of what has transpired within.

Romans 14:17 (NET) says, "For the kingdom of God does not consist of food and drink, but righteousness, peace, and joy in the Holy Spirit." Meaning there is nothing natural about the kingdom of God. It is supernatural in power, dominion, and authority. It is supernatural in righteousness because it is morally correct, decent, and godly. It is peace that cannot be limited or measured. And it is living a life of joy in and through the Holy Spirit.

The joy of the Holy Spirit releases in us so many different emotions and feelings—feelings of calm delight, cheerfulness, gladness, and exceeding joyfulness. Proverbs 17:22 (KJV) tells us, "A merry heart doeth good like a medicine: but a broken spirit drieth the bones." Simply put, a joyful heart can cure the broken in spirit.

Joy is something that must be fully understood in this season. Why? Because joy says that you have reached a place where things don't shake and discourage you like they used to in times past. Joy makes a bold and defiant statement to the enemy, "You no longer intimidate me, because I am walking in the revelation and supernatural understanding that is not of this world."

Application Produces Satisfaction

Application means putting into use what is practical and relevant, closely connected to what is appropriate and present. If we are not relevant and real, we become religious and stagnant, and joy will not thrive where religion dominates (Romans 13:11). We are truly in a critical time where fear, worry, and anxiety dominate thinking and outcomes. Frustration arises when life becomes mundane and ritualistic, leading to complacency and deception. Many fear judgment for any thought of change, yet spiritual stagnation is the result. It's crucial not to spiritually die to be accepted by man.

In personal experience, those demanding the most time and energy are often the least impactful. I spent so much of my life trying to please the people that would eventually abandon me. Managing voices and influences becomes essential for maintaining joy. People demand your time, your energy, and your input, but they rarely apply it to their own lives. Many love God but are bound by doctrine and man-made beliefs, losing true joy. The joy that they had at one time has now all but vanished because they cannot do enough now to be accepted or to please man. Now their joy is gone, and they are mentally exhausted. Applying truth may cost connections, but it releases the Word's power. Application of truth produces satisfaction and allows walking in the comfort of the Holy Spirit.

James 1:22 and 25 urge believers to be doers of the Word, not just hearers, bringing blessings through action. A doer of the Word applies promises and understands that aggression leads to possession. A doer of the Word, or by the Greek word *poiētés*, is one who is a producer, performer, and through obedience, is a fulfiller. This obedience positions believers for God's purpose and fulfills His will. A performer, on the other hand, is someone who shows Jesus by mimicking Jesus. Ultimately as Christians, are we not supposed to be Christlike? Are you a producer, or are you a performer? Spiritual greatness does not come because you are talented. Rather, it comes because you are obedient.

The revelation of these three principles, accompanied with our will to fulfill our individual call and the Great Commission, will afford us the ability to walk, live, and operate in the true joy that the Lord always intended His people to operate in. Here, we walk, live, and operate at a level of accomplishment that allows us to experience the joy of fulfillment.

Romans 8:3–5 emphasizes walking according to the Spirit, setting minds on heavenly things. Our lives revolve around what is most important, valuable, and loved. The most significant aspect should be God and His will, reflecting in actions and reactions. While family, finances, and friends hold importance, sustainable joy comes from a genuine relationship with Jesus. Yes, we are happy when our family is doing well. Yes, there is happiness when our money isn't funny. Yes, we are happy when our relationships with friends are thriving. But the only sustainable and lasting joy comes when we are in the right relationship with the Lord Jesus. Never has time been more precious than it is right now, which calls for urgency to be faithful in this season and hour. Time is fleeting. As one saint used to testify, we have one life to live, and it soon will be passed; what is done for Christ will last.

Ecclesiastes 3:1–8 illustrates life's varied experiences, which our response should align with God's Word. The Hebrew word in this scripture, *èth*, refers to events, experiences, occurrences, and occasions. Life is going to bring us various feelings and emotions. Emotions are instinctive and intuitive feelings that are distinguished from reason or knowledge. Controlling emotions ensures they don't overshadow spiritual identity. Therefore, when we control our emotions instead of our emotions controlling us, we can truly walk in the true joy of the Lord.

We should celebrate accomplishments, birthdays, graduations, and dinners and gifts of acknowledgment, because we are proud of what has taken place. Yes, when life brings tragedy, loss, and the unpredictable, we are to express those feelings accordingly. In that moment, we are emotionally experiencing that. We cannot deny the emotions that come with life, but those feelings and experiences in the natural do not change both who we are and whose we are in the kingdom.

Our emotions do not change who we are, but who we are in the kingdom should empower us on how to respond to any and every situation life brings our way. There is no substitute for experience. That is why experiencing the true joy of the Lord is so vital, especially now. Experiencing the true joy of the Lord will enable us, prepare us, equip us, and even position us.

> *Enable.* To make possible because of the divine authority that has been released to rest on and in every believer.
>
> *Prepare.* To make ready and able to do or deal with anything, everything, anybody and everybody.
>
> *Equip.* To be supplied with the necessary guidance, direction, wisdom to complete and fulfill the purpose to which you have been assigned.
>
> *Position.* To be strategically placed and located in the right and correct place.

Proverbs 4:20–25 emphasizes attending to God's Word and guarding the heart against defilement. There is nothing more important than our obedient response to the Word of God because our initial response is a direct reaction to the revelation we possess and the maturity that we have achieved. Our actions should always reflect the Holy Spirit we possess on the inside. What poetic words from King Solomon, the writer of Proverbs, who instructed us to incline our ears to His sayings, or to prick up the ears, hear, and heed. As believers, it is left up to us to act and keep a careful watch over our feelings and our emotions because of the consistent danger and difficulties that life can and does present, especially now in a nation with seemingly no boundaries or morals. We must guard our hearts to retain and maintain the good and to discard the evil that may try to find its way into it.

Matthew 15:11 reminds us that heart condition reflects spiritual fruit. Believers should produce fruit in line with repentance, commitment, and true joy, which brings inner healing and assurance. Defilement, in a Levitical sense, signifies rendering something unclean, unhallowed, and profane. When we introspect our lives, assessing our conversations, actions, and reactions, we must discern the spiritual fruit we bear, if any. Matthew 3:8 instructs us to produce fruit in line with repentance. Many professing believers fail to exhibit the fruit of commitment, repentance, or true joy despite confessing Jesus as their Savior. Fruit, fundamentally, denotes production and benefit. The fruit of commitment reflects dedication to Christ, while the fruit of repentance signifies a transformed life operating in the spirit. True joy emanates from a heart saturated with God's Word, guarding against false doctrines. It fosters inner healing, confidence, and assurance. Genuine encounters with God and application of scripture yield satisfaction unparalleled by worldly standards. Jesus assures believers in John 16:33 of peace amid tribulations, affirming the indwelling power of the overcomer within us, ensuring we never fall short of victory.

Applying Scripture and encountering the Lord authentically yield satisfaction unparalleled by worldly standards. The true joy of the Lord endures, offering peace amid life's tribulations. As overcomers, believers can walk confidently, fulfilling their purpose in God's kingdom, overcoming, and never underachieving.

CHAPTER 4

No Alignment, No Assignment

Alignment precedes assignment in our lives. Alignment is crucial because it prepares us for God's intended plan and purpose both now and in the future (Psalm 37:23). Through conviction, promptings of the Spirit, and revealed revelation, we begin to understand God's purpose for us. God qualifies the called, and Romans 8:28 reassures us that all things work together for good for those who love God and are called according to His purpose. Never forget that we are all a work in progress. None of us are a finished product yet. And that should excite and ignite every one of us as we continue in our individual and collective journeys.

Change should be more exciting than intimidating. Change means God is not done with you. Embrace God's direction even as He points out your imperfections because He never points out to bring down; He points out to elevate up! He has to clearly reveal to us where we are and what is then available, or we would simply settle for much less.

One of the many things that I have learned is that God will not always show us the big picture but rather snippets of His purpose and plan. Why? Because if He showed us the big picture, we would talk ourselves out of it. We would more than likely become too overwhelmed. Or we would become fixated, overly fascinated, and completely consumed. So He reveals them to us in steps and stages to keep us focused, fervent, grounded, and determined to finish and complete the assignment. This is part of the alignment process: the positioning and the conditioning. The truth is our full completion doesn't manifest until we are all called home to be with our Lord and Savior, Jesus Christ, when mortality puts on immortality. But changing for God is truly freeing and liberating. Aligning to God's will should truly be inspiring and motivating because He truly has our best at heart.

So today I challenge you to embrace your journey. Again, don't rush it and crush it. Live life to its fullest. Refuse to miss a moment. Plan your future, but don't miss enjoying the season! The season you are presently in is all part of the preparation process that gets you to where God desires for you to be. Your struggles will produce His strength! Your hurts will reveal His healing! And your pain will reveal His power! Your alignment will produce His assignment!

Sometimes alignment isn't pretty. In fact, it can be ugly, messy, and uncomfortable because alignment requires being transparent and real. But God will use our past and our present to help sculpt and set up our future. God doesn't need our opinion; God needs our cooperation and cohabitation. Cooperation is our willingness to be led, instructed, and even challenged and changed. Cohabitation is our true, dedicated relationship with the Lord Jesus where we love, honor, and trust His sovereignty and understand He is alive in us to work and to do His will.

I so love John 17:21 (KJV): "That they all may be one; as thou, Father, art in me, and I in thee, that they also may be one in us: that the world may believe that thou hast sent me." It is through cooperation and cohabitation that we all can become as one, just like God the Father and God the Son and God the Holy Spirit are in heaven fulfilling and bringing to fruition the prayer of Jesus. You are truly a called and chosen vessel! You are a vital fixture and a vital part of the plan and purpose of God.

Please know that you weren't just born and then God had to figure out someplace for you to work or some tasks for you to fulfill. There was a need before you, so God created you to fulfill and complete that mission. And I really hope that you will receive this revelation in your heart and spirit. When the Holy Spirit revealed this to me a few years ago, it changed me in so many ways. You were not an accident; you were on purpose! I hope that today, as you are reading this, the Holy Spirit arrests you, and you will live and walk in the complete fullness of this revelation.

So many like me felt different, unique, and not like the others. Not necessarily in a bad way or in a better way, but in a God way. Truthfully, I felt out of place at times because I did feel comfortable in certain settings and places. Things that bothered me, seemingly others were unaffected by. I did not realize that this was all a part of the process of alignment. So my advice to you is simple: never apologize because you are different or because you may look at things from a different perspective. And always remember you have a specific purpose attached to your life.

Personally, I had to realize that God was wanting to do something different in me before He could do something special through me. This is the alignment process. To *align* is "to arrange, position, and place things in the correct order and place for a purpose." So if it feels like the Holy Spirit is working overtime on you, He probably is. Because you are that valuable—you are important to the kingdom of God. The work of the Holy Spirit is to position and prepare us not only for the present but even more so for the future.

This is why alignment is so vitally necessary. Without it, we will never achieve God's intended purpose. You will never stumble into a purpose or trip into a purpose. It will only happen because you are positioning and preparing yourself for it. Alignment takes discipline. And discipline teaches submission. And submission reveals identity and personifies character. In fact, discipline is the practice of training. And we all need godly training, instructing to accomplish the totality of God's plan. Ephesians 4:1 (KJV) says, "I therefore, the prisoner of the Lord, beseech you that ye walk worthy of the vocation wherewith ye are called."

There is nothing more important in the life of any born-again believer than genuine heart-inspired spirit-led commitment to the call of God on their lives. And the Bible says that each of us must be responsible enough to walk worthy or appropriately in the position wherewith they have been called. It's one thing to accept a call, but it takes application, dedication, and a willingness to pursue the call and then to be sold out to complete the call. This is where a level of responsibility comes into play. There is a code of conduct that must be properly followed. This code of conduct requires disciplined obedience and proper behavior.

It's an awesome thing to be free but a dangerous thing to be without borders and perimeters. Spiritual freedom and liberation will produce and release an unlimited level of joy and peace in the life of a child of God. And it is this type of joy that is satisfying and gratifying to the individual and attractive to onlookers. It is a way of witnessing our faith and showing that God has a plan for every person despite their past. The anointing and gifting you possess are appealing, but to protect what you have, you must guard and protect the doorway of your heart from deception, heartbreak, and limiting beliefs that can steal the joy from your life.

There are what I call buzzkills. You were having a great day. Things were going good and then suddenly, people who do not possess the true joy of the Lord and are not in alignment with God come into your life. This can be friends, or this can be family. Sadly, family too often can be the most destructive and devastating because of the genetic connection. And I know when it comes to family, we want to fix, solve, and troubleshoot, mend, heal, and restore what is broken. But part of living in the joy of the Lord is learning how to let go and surrender them over to the Lord. If you do not, your joy will never be full because your life will be consumed with the weightiness that was not your responsibility to carry in the first place.

Your response and actions come from the things you think and believe. If you have the right beliefs in your heart, your actions will be life-giving, life-changing, and life-motivating. As you move in the right direction, it will cause your heart to remain right and pure. As you obey and consistently apply the Word of God to your life, you will experience what the true joy of the Lord really is. But if your heart is impure, you will do things with the wrong motives. God cannot bless what we have chosen to curse through disobedience!

So in this alignment process, guard your heart, guard your conversation, and guard your mind. In doing so, you will continue to position and condition yourself for God's plan to come into alignment that will release your personal and individual assignment. The book of Proverbs 18:27 sheds and reveals some amazing standards to go by as we are on this journey of life. In fact, I would even go so far as to say that it is truly a lifeline for every believer to receive and live their lives by.

Proverbs 4:24–27 (NIV) says, "Keep your mouth free of perversity; keep corrupt talk far from your lips. Let your eyes look straight ahead; fix your gaze directly before you. Give careful thought to the paths for your feet and be steadfast in all your ways. Do not turn to the right or the left; keep your foot from evil." Wrong conversations will lead to negligence and wrong interpretations, misinformation, and wrong judgment of character. Wrong interpretations can lead to misleading deception. And negligence can too often hold back and disqualify a person from the totality of God's plan. We must do as Scripture has said: we must "fix our gaze" directly before us. The term *fix your gaze* means "to steadily look straight ahead, unchanging in your direction."

Of course, this is referring to our spiritual focus where we choose to remain unshaken in our focus and unmoved in our determination because we refuse to waver or get off course. This is significant in this hour when compromise has become the normal instead of the abnormal. When spiritual commitment is seemingly outdated and not with the times. When being spiritually faithful is not such a big deal anymore. Could it be that the reason many today who claim to be religious find themselves seldom pursuing their identity and purpose in Christ?

Sadly, so many have a form of godliness, but they deny His true power, like 2 Timothy 3:5 prophesies. You can call me old-fashioned, but I still believe in being sold out and faithful to God. I want my personal walk with him to have purpose and meaning. I want to make sure that I am properly aligning myself to the Word of God. I am sure that you feel much like me in that you want to make sure that your energy and effort hits its mark and has significant impact.

This is your life; make the best of it! Don't waste it on things that just demand your time, but don't pay back a spiritual dividend.

Proverbs 4:23 states, "Keep thy heart with all diligence, for out of it are the issues of life." This incredible word instructs us all to carefully watch and monitor our hearts. Why? Because potential defilement is always lingering and lurking. Our hearts, both naturally and spiritually, are our lifeline! Through our heart, our lives are lived. Therefore, a strong heart will lead to a productive life.

I encourage you to guard your heart, pursue the plan God has for you, and make sure your decisions are biblically based and spirit-led, and as a result, great things are going to happen. The Word of God will help you know what belongs in your heart and what doesn't. You are to carefully always weigh your heart to ensure it remains pure. Your heart is your life because your life is directed by what is in your heart. Keeping your heart with diligence means that you will only allow into it what will help you become more godly, more loving, and more confident. Your heart has the issues or details of your life, and that is why it is hard to live a joyful life with a broken heart, and the enemy knows that.

Jesus came to heal the brokenhearted. We all have had our hearts broken, but He is the mender and healer so that we all can live a full, concentrated, and productive life.

CHAPTER 5

Passing the Test

All spiritual attacks, whether carnal or spiritual, must be combatted, confronted, and met with "a spirit of joy." Joy reveals that our identity and our chemistry in the Lord is intact and at work in our life. It reveals an inner strength and signifies that we have come to a place of spiritual understanding and promise where nothing separates or comes between God's peace, promise, and provision for our lives.

Testing and persecution are inevitable; it's going to happen, but it's how we respond that determines the outcome. "Blessed are ye when men shall revile you, and persecute you, and shall say all manner of evil against you falsely, for my sake. Rejoice and be glad [or possess joy] because your reward is great in heaven, for they persecuted the prophets before you in the same way."

Revile, by definition, is "to be critical and abusive in an insulting manner." *Persecute*, by definition, is "to harass or annoy someone persistently." Passing the test doesn't mean punching someone in the face or giving someone a piece of your mind. Passing the test is when our response reveals our maturity, our experience, and our true heart.

Through whom we have also obtained access by faith into this grace in which we stand, and we rejoice in the hope of God's glory. Therefore, we can also rejoice in suffering, knowing that suffering produces, yields, and supplies. You do not know just how strong you are until you find yourself in a spiritual test.

This brings you great joy, though now for a season, if need be, you are in heaviness, grief, and distress through manifold temptations or tests. *Test*—evaluate!

> *Test*—nominate
> *Test*—graduate

On a sidenote, it is incredibly important, because if we do not pass the test, then we fail the class! If we fail the class, we must take the course over. This is why our attitude, our perception, and our conception of the truth are so valuable and indispensable. It brings order to chaos and joy to sorrow. And with the consistent and persistent increase and elevation of spiritual warfare in this hour, the joy of the Lord is truly going to be our strength.

Titles are no good without discipline and training. The truth is we are all going to get wounded and offended because the enemy will see to it. He will want you to blame something or someone for holding you back, when the truth is you just failed the test. Here is the reality: we all have passed tests, and we all have failed tests! But whether we passed or failed, we can never stop growing, maturing, and moving.

Tests reveal the heart and the fight of someone. Tests expose weaknesses, and tests expose strengths! I am convinced that people do not know just how strong and resilient they are until they are in a battle that tests who they really are! Truthfully, we all need to encounter battles and tests because both are essential.

Both are incredibly vital. Why? For the development of character, personality, and purpose. Our character is our personality traits. Character is what reveals the real you. And when tests come, the real you will manifest. When tests come, the real you comes to the forefront to confront what is opposing you.

The real you will always shine. The real you will be exposed, whether good or bad. In every trial and every obstacle we face, when we do not allow the Holy Spirit to handle them, we will never hit our mark, intention, or purpose. It is only when we choose not to submit to His authority, power, direction, and jurisdiction that we fail or walk in defeat.

This is why we must consistently remind ourselves that we have been purchased with the precious blood of the Lord Jesus, who gives us the power, the dominion, and authority to operate and navigate in the divine peace and benefit of the Holy Spirit.

Psalm 37:23–24 (KJV) says, "The steps of a good man are ordered by the LORD: And he delights in his way. Though he falls, he shall not be utterly cast down: For the LORD upholds him with his hand." James 1:3–4 (KJV) says, "Knowing this, that the trying of your faith works patience. But let patience have her perfect work, that ye may be perfect and entire, wanting nothing." True battles reveal! True battles unveil! True battles often reveal what has been previously concealed!

"For though we walk in the flesh, we do not war after the flesh." Too often, people want to put a face with their problem. But a lot of the time, it is not a person as much as it is a spirit that is behind it. And if we can identify the spirit, we can identify the real problem at hand. And if we can truly unveil the real issue, then we can deal with it properly and pass the test.

Ephesians 6:12–13 tells us, "For we wrestle not against flesh and blood, but against principalities, against powers, against the rulers of the darkness of this world, against spiritual wickedness in high places. Wherefore take unto you the whole armor of God, that ye may be able to withstand in the evil day, and having done all, to stand."

We contend against principalities. The Bible expressed that principalities are the demonic hierarchy that attempts to produce anarchy in our spiritual walk with God. This is where spiritual attacks escalate into full-blown spiritual warfare. I need to challenge someone that there were some things that tried to and even succeeded in attaching to you that must not permit to follow you into your new season.

The apostle Paul said in Philippians 3:13–14, "Brethren, I count not myself to have apprehended [understood or perceived], but this one thing I do, forgetting those things which are behind, and reaching forth unto the things which are before, I press toward the mark for the prize of the high calling of God in Christ Jesus." Paul was saying, "I had to take a step back and realize I do not have it all together yet, but what is behind me is behind me, and that is where it needs to stay! And what is in front of me is my opportunity to achieve my destiny and I am going to press and push and run swiftly to catch and obtain that, that I was created for."

I love the fact that Paul used the word *forgetting* to describe one of the actions he was going to take in the season he was in. *Forgetting* means "to lose out of one's mind"! Not "to lose one's mind" but "to lose out of one's mind" where it no longer has the power or ability to confine, produce fear and worry, or paralyze the vision! You know, retrospection is not a bad thing when you survey or review a past course, event, or period in your life if you do not allow it to overwhelm you but let it cause you to grow and learn!

We must refuse to be defined by our past but rather by our present and our future! Spiritual wisdom says: step back and reflect, step back and evaluate, and step back and conclude. When we reflect, we are then thinking deeply and carefully about the decisions we made and the conclusions that we came to. When we evaluate, we can properly access the value of something and form a better understanding of its worth. And finally, when we conclude, we are then able to come to a decision and must ask ourselves "Have we made the right judgment, and have we formed the right opinion?"

The church needs to take a step back and revisit and recalibrate what it takes to be a true follower and disciple of Christ! In Luke 14, we are told that great crowds were following Jesus. His popularity was growing. He was the talk of the town. Miracles were manifesting, and healings were occurring almost everywhere He went. It was right amid all these supernatural releases that Jesus begins to disciple and lay out terms for being a true disciple and follower of him because there were so many who were wanting to follow Him.

I am seeing more and more that people want the glory, the signs, the wonders, and the power of the Holy Spirit; but they do not want to be discipled! You cannot help anyone if they think they know more than you or think they are more spiritual than you are! It is interesting to me that right during His glory days with the huge crowds, the accolades, the adoration, and the notoriety, He stayed focused, committed, and determined to His assignment. Jesus began to talk and teach them about discipleship, because the Bible said that He knew their hearts! He knew they desired the benefits of what He did rather than a true understanding of who He was. People today want the benefits and blessings of God without a sold-out commitment and dedication to God! Passing the test is much more than attending a weekly religious church service. It is about understanding the price Jesus paid for our sins. It is about us understanding our responsibility as followers of Jesus, plain and simple.

Matthew 16:24–26 (KJV) says, "Then said Jesus unto his disciples, If any man will come after me, let him deny himself, and take up his cross, and follow me. For whosoever will save his life shall lose it: and whosoever will lose his life for my sake shall find it. For what is a man profited, if he shall gain the whole world, and lose his own soul? or what shall a man give in exchange for his soul?" Jesus begins to disciple his disciples by first explaining what it was going to take to be one of His followers. The first thing Jesus said was that we had to deny ourselves and take up our cross. The word *deny* that Jesus used is very demanding and accountable. It literally means "to forget oneself; to lose sight of oneself and one's own interests." That seems like a whole lot for someone to ask of another person, doesn't it?

When the person who is asking it is the one who has already given up a lot and is also about to lay down his life for the sins of all humanity, well, it now takes on a whole new perspective, doesn't it? Denial here refers to the controlling of the flesh. The flesh is the enemy of the spirit. You will never accomplish the will of God and the purpose of God if you don't control your flesh and get it under subjection. Truthfully, whoever controls the flesh controls the destiny. This is why that the denial of one's flesh is so significant and profound.

Jesus said that his followers would have to deny or disown themselves and take up their cross and wholeheartedly follow him. The cross was a symbol of suffering, death, shame, and ridicule. When the genuine followers of Jesus take up their cross, they are taking control of their life. They are making a statement to heaven and to hell that they have decided, and that decision is, "I am following Jesus wherever He leads me because He is the Way, the Truth, and the Life."

I know that will be honored by heaven when I am ridiculed for the name of the Lord's sake. I am blessed when they say all manner of evil against me. In fact, I am passing the test of life because I have obtained the revelation that Jesus is my Source and my Hope. Be encouraged and know that tests are a part of your journey. They are essential for you to see His will in the earth. Be encouraged and even inspired because tests reveal and expose what had been previously hidden.

Always know that we serve a very mindful God who is touched with our feelings and emotions. He is our faithful friend. Our comfort and strength in the difficulties of life come what may. I love what the prophet Isaiah said in Isaiah 40:28–31 (NLT): "Have you never heard? Have you never understood? The Lord is the everlasting God, the Creator of all the earth. He never grows weak or weary. No one can measure the depths of his understanding. He gives power to the weak and strength to the powerless. Even youths will become weak and tired, and young men will fall in exhaustion. But those who trust in the Lord will find new strength. They will soar high on wings like eagles. They will run and not grow weary. They will walk and not faint."

Count it all joy no matter the circumstance or situation because He is an ever-present help. He is a supernatural phenomenon. And because of who He is, you will become who you were born to be. Remember, other people do not define you! You must define yourself! Don't attempt to fit in when you were called and anointed to stand out! Don't suppress who you are, but boldly profess and possess who you are in Christ Jesus.

I wish I could tell you that the attacks are going to end, but they aren't, and that is okay because God has not forgotten you. He is mindful of you, and He is fighting for you. In Isaiah 54:17 (NIV), we are assured, "No weapon forged against you will prevail, and you will refute every tongue that accuses you. This is the heritage of the servants of the Lord, and this is their vindication from me,' declares the Lord."

Fight the good fight of faith. Don't let up, slow down, or give ground. Let the passion you display be derived from the hunger you have inside! Because I have good news for you. You and the Lord have got this, and what the enemy meant for evil, God is turning for His good.

CHAPTER 6

Joy Was Never Intended to Be Seasonal

We all possess a common thread. That common thread is that we all face the positives and the negatives of life. But it is how we face them that ultimately determines the outcome.

Sadly, today people have gotten so accustomed to the negative that try to consume and even dominate that they hardly ever expect the positive to occur and manifest. There will never be a positive explosion unless there has first come a supernatural implosion. Allow me to explain this. An implosion is what occurs inside the believer that releases and allows a spiritual explosion to manifest outside the believer. The word *implosion* means "a violent occurrence on the inside." All the while, the word *explosion* means there has been a violent occurrence on the outside. *Explosion* means there has been a detonation, eruption, and igniting of something that had been previously contained. Truly, there needs to be an implosion of joy to the believer so that there can an explosion of that joy to a dying world that is seeking help and in dire need of hope.

The world thinks that joy is in accumulations, prestige, position, and prominence. This is the masquerading lie that is being preached, promulgated, and promoted by corporate America. It is nothing more than a smoke screen and a deceptive lie that consumes and dominates the mind and hearts of people, because they think that there is a pot of gold at the end of the rainbow they are chasing. Jesus was very clear in John 16:33 (NIV). "I have told you these things, so that in me you may have peace. In this world you will have trouble. But take heart! I have overcome the world." The world can only produce lies, deception, and trouble; and Jesus made that very clear.

But He also made it very clear that as believers, we can take heart, because He has overcome the world. The term *take heart* means "to take courage and be confident and be hopeful." I would submit that we could also add "to walk in confident joy."

The joy that the Lord gave his people was never intended to be limited by the cares of life or derailed by the attacks of life. True joy is revelatory because it means that there has been a true understanding that His joy is not of this world. And since it is not of this world, it cannot be affected or infected by this world. True joy is from above, and it is not earthly. Therefore, it is not conditional. The true joy of the Lord should be perpetual. *Perpetual* means that it is everlasting, never-ending, eternal, permanent, unending, and endless. So I would submit to you that godly joy is the key to true peace of mind. Godly joy will sustain you when the trials of life attack you.

Joy is an expression of what is truly taking place in the life of a believer. Joy makes a statement about our relationship with the Lord. It is evident that our adversary hates our joy in the Lord, or he wouldn't battle and fight it like he does. Our enemy knows just how attractive the joy of the Lord really is to others around us. How inspiring and encouraging it is!

Proverbs 3:13 (KJV) states, "Happy is the man that findeth wisdom, and the man that getteth understanding." The word *happy* used in Proverbs 3:13 means "blessed and fortunate." To find wisdom here means to secure it, acquire it, and get it. To get understanding to obtain intelligence and insight. So joy and happiness are obtainable, but according to Scripture, you have to go after it and then learn to live it.

I read something that said, "Happiness, joy, and praising God seems to evade our thinking when life gets crazy! Even when life is running along smoothly, it is easy to totally forget to praise God in the mundane of our lives." We must determine to walk in joy. Joy must be an expression of what is truly manifesting in our life. Allow me to take it a little farther. It doesn't matter how long you have been saved or even filled with the Holy Spirit. The truth is that true joy ultimately comes from a disciplined lifestyle. Discipline comes when there is a sold-out focus.

Focus occurs when there is nothing else that competes with what is most important in your life. You can be saved and still not fully walk in the true joy of the Lord. You can teach a Sunday school class and still not fully walk in the true joy of the Lord. You can pastor a church or be a youth pastor, worship leader, or skilled musician and still not fully walk in the true joy of the Lord. Friend, *joy was never intended to be seasonal.*

In Psalm 34:1, we read, "I will praise the Lord at all times; His praise will always be on my lips." The words *all times* in this context refers to spiritual discipline and spiritual maturity. Allow me to quickly define:

> *Discipline* involves the practice, application and training of our mind and our lifestyle to mark up and to obey the word.
> *Discipline* is controlled behavior that embraces correction.

Psalm 34:5 states, "Those who look to Him are radiant with joy; their faces will never be ashamed." Joyful people beam with light. They are inspiring, elevating, and motivating. They instill hope, help, and comfort. Joy in a born-again believer should never be seasonal.

In the hour that we live in, there are a lot of people who are dealing with incredible fear, worry, and anxiety. The world is filled with great concern about what is next. And if the church is just as consumed as the world is, then we are going to miss a great opportunity for a harvest of souls.

We read in 1 Peter 1:8, "You have not seen him, but you love him. You do not see Him now, but you believe in Him, and so you rejoice with an indescribable and glorious joy." Truly, the joy of the

Lord is indescribable. It is beyond words. It is beyond definition, but it is real. It is tangible, and it is obtainable.

> **Question:** With the life you live, the actions you portray, and conversation from your mouth, would anybody say that you have the joy of the Lord?

I know that is rather straightforward and to the point, but as believers, we are either leading people *to* God or potentially leading them *from* God.

Joy is one of the greatest witnessing tools any believer ever possessed because in a very negative, unsure, and insecure world, people are looking for some ray of hope and relief. Displaying and showing joy can motivate those around us to inquire why and how we possess so much happiness and joy. You do not have to have a special calling or gifting to be a soul winner. Just be completely in love with Jesus and show what true joy is all about, and the Holy Spirit can do the rest. Joy is not limited or rationed but is distributed liberally, freely, and equally to all who call on the name of the Lord.

I titled this chapter "Joy Was Never Intended to Be Seasonal" because even as born-again believers, if we are not disciplined, focused, and determined, we can fall into the same mundane trap as the world. The trap of always wanting acceptance, affirmation, and conformation. The trap of "not good enough." The trap of never possessing enough. The trap of frustration. These are all real feelings and emotions that can become so consuming and dominating that joy, in many, becomes seasonal and inconsistent. Are you tired of seasonal joy? Do you find yourself even frustrated because you know that you do not possess the joy you need and the joy you should possess?

Well, I have some good gospel news for you: you can *have* the joy of the Lord, but not only that, you can also *maintain* and *keep* the joy of the Lord. "How?" you may ask. By going to the Word of God and studying and applying its precious promises. We serve a God of promises; therefore, as His children, we can live in those promises. Hebrews 10:23 says, "Let us hold fast the profession of our faith without wavering; (for he is faithful that promised)." Please note the importance of our profession. *Profession* is our declaration. And what kind of declaration are you making?

Filter your words. Filter your conversation because by doing so, you can control your destination. Words are so powerful. Our words either release us or confine us. Mark 11:23 says, "For verily I say unto you, that whosoever shall say unto this mountain, Be thou removed, and be thou cast into the sea; and shall not doubt in his heart, but shall believe that those things which he saith shall come to pass; he shall have whatsoever he saith."

Our words can change and alter our present position and condition. Stand firm. In Galatians 5:1 (KJV), we are told, "Stand fast therefore in the liberty wherewith Christ hath made us free, and be not entangled again with the yoke of bondage." Please note that at the very beginning of this verse, the apostle Paul says to *stand fast*, or it could be rendered *stand firm*, which indicates and makes a statement about the foundation.

The higher the structure, the deeper the foundation. No matter how good the materials are, a building is only as sure as its foundation. The word *stand* indicates position. Position projects intention, and intention reveals purpose and plan. So to stand fast and firm means you know who you are and where you are going. Please note how Paul warns about repeat entanglement. Entanglement is the Greek word *enéchō*, which refers to so many different feelings, responses, and emotions that, if not dealt with, will not only consume us but even dictate whether we will have a full life or not.

Entanglement deals with the things that ensnare, consume, and dominate us. Holding a grudge produces entanglement because you allow that hurt, that wound, or even that grief to dictate and dominate how you feel, how you respond, and even how you love. Entanglements trap and ensnare freedom, and freedom is one of the great qualities that salvation bestowed upon all believers of Christ. Another great quality of God's grace is that we do not have to be slaves bound by the entangling chains of hurt, regret, and failure because who the Son sets free is truly free indeed.

Joy was never intended to be seasonal. And in a perfect world, it would be a lot easier. Of course, we do not live in a perfect world, but we serve a perfect God who placed His Spirit within us, as believers, that is flawless. If we submit, commit, and then transmit what we possess and allow Him to lead, guide, and navigate our steps, our thoughts, and our words, we will certainly live a more fulfilled and successful life.

His joy was never intended to be seasonal but always continual, because we can walk in His promise, His fulfillment, and His joy that allows us to enjoy a fulfilled and prosperous life. How about you? Do you walk in perpetual joy or seasonal joy? Is your joy based upon life, or is your life based upon joy? Great questions, aren't they? This is truly one of the main reasons why I feel the Holy Spirit challenged me to write this book, because we all face those times when we struggle to live in His full joy. Why? Because life can be so demanding, draining, and at times, straining. So many deadlines, responsibilities, and accountabilities can take their toll on all of us.

Truthfully, we can be depleted and even be defeated by its endless demand. This is where we must stop allowing life to dominate us and, instead, begin to dominate it.

Simply allow His joy to rule and reign in our life. In all reality, isn't life way too short to not enjoy it? And if you are not enjoying life, well, you can change it. "This is the day that the Lord hath made, I will rejoice and be glad in it" (Psalm 118:24). This declaration encapsulates the essence of embracing joy as a deliberate choice, even amid life's complexities and challenges. As believers, we are called to embody joy not as a fleeting emotion but as an enduring state of being rooted in our faith and trust in God's promises.

The journey to perpetual joy requires a conscious commitment to align our thoughts, words, and actions with the truth of God's Word. It necessitates a steadfast resolve to stand firm in our faith, refusing to be entangled by the snares of doubt, fear, and negativity. By anchoring ourselves in the unwavering love and grace of Christ, we can transcend the limitations of seasonal joy and embrace the abundant life that He has promised.

So I challenge you to reflect on your journey. Are you content with seasonal joy, or are you ready to embrace the fullness of joy that God offers? The choice is yours. Let us strive together to walk in the joy of the Lord, not just for a season, but for all the days of our lives.

May the joy of the Lord be your strength, guiding you through every season and circumstance, and may it shine forth as a beacon of hope and inspiration to a world in need of light. Amen.

CHAPTER 7

Joy That Comes from Submissive Discipleship

I know that this is a very interesting title for a chapter in a book, but there is so much truth in the title itself. Simply because one of the most neglected things in the Church is true solid Scripture-based discipleship that creates understanding, comprehension, and cognitive apprehension. Understanding that reveals what can only be revealed through the revelation of the Holy Spirit, comprehension of the things that are not on the surface can only be obtained through the revelation of the Holy Spirit, and apprehension or the grasping of the revelation of truth through the revelation of the Holy Spirit.

Spiritual growth and maturity are not only for your spiritual benefit and well-being, but also to benefit those you are trying to lead, inspire, and influence those you want to lead to Jesus. Spiritual growth and maturity strategically position and condition us to live effective and efficient lives, creating atmospheres that change outcomes and circumstances. True discipleship brings light to so many things that are game changers when the truth of the Word is dissected and projected.

Allow me to better express the statement and what I mean. When something is dissected, it is cut up into smaller pieces for better consumption and digestion. When something is dissected, it is analyzed, examined, and studied. It is here where discussion can be made available for authenticity, accountability, and availability. When something is dissected, it is better understood; therefore, it will be more likely to be received and consequently applied. To *dissect* means to bring to life piece by piece, which is exactly what discipleship does.

The second part is projection. When something is projected, it is, in fact, revealing not only the cost of something but also the potential value of something. Everything in life has checks and balances. Therefore, if we are not willing to embrace spiritual checks and balances, then we will never know what is truly available to us as born-again believers.

This brings me to the theme and intention of this book, *Count It All Joy*, because it is in the revelation of who we are in Christ through the Holy Spirit teaching us that we can have the true joy of the Lord during great tests, attacks, and trials. The presence of the Lord brings such joy to the lives of His people, but discipleship elevates the individual to better understand and comprehend the depth of joy that all believers can possess and access.

I am so concerned that many professing believers are not being properly discipled, either because it is not being offered where they attend or because there is a failure on the part of the hearer, who is not willing to be a submissive applier of what is being taught. True discipleship not only reveals what is available, but also it will reveal any type of potential deception.

When Jesus was sitting with His disciples on the Mount of Olives in Matthew 24, they ask Him what the end would look like or, in other words, how we will know the end-times are upon us. And in Matthew 24:4 (KJV), we read, "And Jesus answered and said unto them, Take heed that no man deceive you!" *Deceive* is the Greek word *planáō*, which means "to cause to stray, to lead astray, to lead aside from the right way, to wander, and to roam about." Again, in Matthew 24:11 (KJV) Jesus said, "And many false prophets shall rise, and shall deceive many." First Corinthians 3:18 (KJV) has, "Let no man deceive himself. If any man among you seemeth to be wise in this world, let him become a fool, that he may be wise." In James 1:22–25 (KJV), it is written, "But be ye doers of the word, and not hearers only, deceiving your own selves. For if any be a hearer of the word, and not a doer, he is like unto a man beholding his natural face in a glass: for he beholdeth himself, and goeth his way, and straightway forgetteth what manner of man he was." There are so many more verses in Scripture that make known the danger and destruction of deception.

We are seeing such a decline in godliness and righteousness when it comes to the twenty-first-century Church, and it concerns me. *Holiness* is a word seldom heard anymore in the pulpits of corporate America. It is not accepted or wanted by many because it means a life change, a goal change, and a priority change. Sadly, many are being indoctrinated to conform to a religious standard, but they are not being equipped and prepared for what can be accomplished and achieved in them in the kingdom of God.

So many have things, but they don't have joy. They have degrees, but they don't have joy. They have careers, but they don't have joy. They have money, but they don't have joy. Jesus is very clear in Matthew 6:33 (KJV), "But seek ye first the kingdom of God, and his righteousness; and all these things shall be added unto you." This is not a suggestion, but a command and declaration of the Lord Jesus concerning the sequential way that all believers and followers of Jesus are to pursue and navigate.

You will always pursue what is most important and significant in your life. And this is where discipleship releases the revelation of joy that should flood the hearts and minds of every follower of Jesus. It is one thing to be saved, but it is another thing to have the joy of the Lord. Again, the main theme of this book is "count it all joy."

I want you, right now, to simply ask yourself these questions: "Am I happy?" "Am I enjoying life?" "Do I possess the true joy of the Lord?" "And do I show it, express it, and convey it?" These are somewhat simple yet significant questions that we must ask ourselves in order to get a proper grasp on the reality and truth of true joy.

Are you one of those people who experience seasonal joy and occasional joy? Are you one of them who find yourself seemingly on a spiritual roller coaster of highs and lows? This is seasonal joy and occasional joy. And this certainly is not the will of God.

How do we obtain continual joy instead of experiencing seasonal joy and occasional joy? Well, I am glad you ask! It is through personal and corporate disciplined discipleship and training that produces who Jesus really is in you through the working of the Holy Spirit. When a believer allows the Holy Spirit to truly come alive in them it is a true game changer for them for the rest of their lives.

Because He is "the Spirit of Truth" meaning that He is absolute Truth. Isaiah describes Him this way in Isaiah 11:2 (NET): "The Lord's spirit will rest on him—a spirit that gives extraordinary wisdom, a spirit that provides the ability to execute plans, a spirit that produces absolute loyalty to the Lord." Wow! I love this so much because it is the validity and validation of this truth that promises true joy.

As born-again believers, we must fully know and grasp that the Lord's Spirit rests on us as believers. His Spirit grants us extraordinary wisdom and the ability to execute plans! And the Spirit produces in us absolute loyalty to the Lord. *Extraordinary wisdom* is unmatched wisdom, remarkable wisdom, exceptional wisdom, amazing wisdom, and astonishing and astounding wisdom.

It goes on and on, but I think you get the point. The ability to execute plans assures us that through the Holy Spirit we will make sound decisions, precise resolutions, and successful interpretations. *Absolute loyalty* means that through the Holy Spirit, we can and will walk in stability, availability, and accountability. All this ensures and enables us to walk in consistent and even perpetual joy because we have disciplined ourselves to walk and navigate that way. It becomes learned behavior because we have learned like the apostle Paul that whatever state we find ourselves in, we are content (Philippians 4:11 KJV).

Second Corinthians 4:7 (KJV) tells us, "But we have this treasure in earthen vessels, that the excellency of the power may be of God, and not of us." The treasure we possess as believers is not in external accumulations, but our treasure is within us. Success can never be associated with the external because those are things, possessions, and purchases that can and will lose value.

True success is the development of what is within first, which will certainly manifest outwardly. Joy doesn't come from accumulations as much as it comes from associations, meaning my connection to God through diligent development of my walk in the Holy Spirit far outweighs anything I can monetarily accumulate, obtain, or accomplish. Things are superficial fillers that cannot bring true joy. Only the peace of God's promises, provision, and steadfastness can do that.

I have great concern because of the busyness of life that is so consuming and demanding; it robs people of valuable time that cannot be retrieved. Seemingly, time has accelerated to the point where it is as though you now need twenty-five hours a day because twenty-four is not enough to get done what you need to get done. Our days are planned before we even wake up, and we go at breakneck speed to get them done, only to be so exhausted from a grueling day that has now taken much of the night to get done.

It is hard to have joy when you are exhausted. It is hard to think clearly or make proper decisions when you are fatigued. It is hard to be faithful to God when the demand is so great on our life. Yes, as parents, grandparents, etc., we want to ensure that our children enjoy the life that we did not get to when we were young. Yes, we want them to have the things that we never had, but what are we really teaching them? We are teaching them, or should I say disciplining them, to allow whatever is deemed important naturally to take the place of what should be the most important, and that is being a disciplined disciple of Jesus Christ. This is where actions speak louder than words.

We all must be guilty of being disciplined, determined, and dedicated to the will, way, and call of the Lord Jesus. This is where discipleship is so significant and valuable. The teachings of Jesus are so incredibly humbling, inviting, and defining because He taught as one who legitimately cared. He taught by showing genuine love. He taught by well-released passionate words. He taught forgiveness and then demonstrated it on the cross. He taught healing and then performed them. He was not all words, but His words carried weight. He knew the importance of demonstration, not just bland conversation.

The First Epistle of John 3:18 states, "My little children, let us not love in word, neither in tongue; but in deed and in truth." John was not saying that words weren't important, but rather that words without action are futile and a waste. To love indeed reveals the real heart, the real motive, and the intention.

Jesus taught that the kingdom of heaven is for those who willingly humble themselves. Those who are teachable, patient, and long-suffering. Jesus said, "Be ye therefore merciful, as your Father also is merciful" (Luke 6:36), meaning those who show mercy will also receive mercy. There is incredible power in our words! Our words are expressions of maturity or the lack thereof. Our words reveal our past and our destination. Our words express where we are currently at and where we are going. Words release blessing or cursing. The Bible said in Matthew 12:37 that by our words we are justified (acquitted) and by our words we are condemned (unrighteous). Reckless and unseasoned words are undisciplined words that lead to disastrous outcomes and hurt feelings. A person's conversation will reveal where they are going and who they are connected to.

What about you? How does your conversation usually begin? Are you positive, motivating, and encouraging? Or do you begin a conversation from a defensive posture?

A defensive posture means to begin your conversation from a place of past hurt that has not been healed; therefore, you feel you must always be guarded, protective, and controlling. A defensive posture reveals that the true joy of the Lord is not presently active or dominant. Truthfully, a defensive posture is exactly the posture the enemy wants us to have because it in no way glorifies God. It is not attractive, but distractive. It's not the right portrayal of who a believer is supposed to represent or display. A defensive posture intercepts joy. In fact, I would suggest to you that true joy is not present at all where a defensive posture dominates and reigns.

Fictional joy, simply put, is fake joy. Fake joy will never take the place of true joy. Joy comes through experience, encounter, and understanding. Experience is when you obtain firsthand knowledge, training, learning, education, wisdom, professionalism, and sophistication. An encounter is an experience where you come face-to-face with something. Understanding refers to our comprehension, apprehension, full grasp through perception, discernment, appreciation, and interpretation. Understanding also reveals our level of spiritual conception, digestion, assimilation, absorption, knowledge, awareness, consciousness, and our insight. True knowledge is the power to truly know firsthand and personally who the Lord really is, not based upon someone else's interpretation and revelation but one that is based upon our own personal encounter and experience.

The Bible said in Daniel 11:32, "And such as do wickedly against or toward the covenant shall he corrupt by flatteries: but the people that do know their God shall be strong, and do exploits or they will display strength, they will act, and they will accomplish great things."

CHAPTER 8

The Balance of Joy

The word *balance* is defined as "an even distribution of weight enabling someone or something to remain upright and steady." I chose the title "The Balance of Joy" because I believe with everything in me that not only is our nation at a very crucial and pivotal point, but likewise the Church is at a very crucial and pivotal point at this time in human history. I say that because there seems to be an absence of balance in both. Without balance, there cannot be true and lasting joy.

Balance is when things equal out. Balance is when we learn and even choose to truly live a whole and complete life that is filled with discipline, joy, and happiness. Balance is knowing who you are in Christ Jesus. Balance is based on a solid spiritual relationship with the Lord that is based upon experience, encounter, and faith.

> *Experience* is willful submission to training that produces a release of education, learning, and knowledge that leads to maturity.
>
> *Encounter* is an experience that is so life-changing that it cannot be questioned or doubted.
>
> *Faith* is complete trust and confidence that releases promise, provision, and destiny.

We must make the best out of life. And for anyone to take life for granted and not daily pursue and develop their walk with Jesus will only produce a life that is out of balance, out of control. It will produce a life that will come short of the glory of the Lord. It will be a life that is mediocre at best. Our decisions have consequences and repercussions not only for the present but for the future. Our decisions do not just affect us, but everything connected and associated to us, not to mention the generations to follow.

We live in a time of immense distraction and negligence, and both distraction and negligence are the small foxes that will destroy the potential grapes on the vine. Distractions are strategic in design to get and even keep the focus on what should be the true focal point of focus. Negligence is the byproduct and offspring of distraction. The more distracted you become, the more negligent you will be, and the enemy knows this. This is why he created the distraction to begin with. The enemy knows that he cannot defeat a Christian because Jesus gave the believer power over all the power of the enemy.

In Luke 10:19 (KJV), we read, "Behold, I give unto you power to tread on serpents and scorpions, and over all the power of the enemy: and nothing shall by any means hurt you." Since the enemy knows he cannot defeat us, he tries to cause us to defeat ourselves by self-destructing. How? Through forfeiting our purpose and not developing our spiritual walk.

Sadly, the cares and snares of life have got so many distracted that many no longer have time for God or His work. They have no balance of life. They have no concept of what is truly being willfully surrendered by their actions or the lack thereof. They are consumed more and more with their plans, their wishes, and their agendas. What is sad is that they seemingly don't even realize it. That is scary to say the least. Negligence has become a silent assassin that will lead to spiritual depravity. Temporal gratification will never sustain lasting joy because it doesn't possess the means or the ability to do so.

The fulfillment of flesh cannot sustain, nor can it maintain the lasting joy that can only come from a true, sold-out, and dedicated relationship with the Lord Jesus. In fact, the only thing that is lasting and eternal is the joy of the Lord through a consecrated relationship with Him. Joy is not earthly accumulations as much as it is heavenly accommodations. Because, what the earth provides is temporal and what heaven provides is eternal. What we need is balance.

It is interesting that the symbol of our court system is called *Lady Justice*. She got her origin in Rome. Her posture and position with the scales is to restore balance and fairness to society. The scales that Lady Justice holds represent and symbolize the impartiality of the court's decision, and the sword she holds symbolizes the power of justice. The reason the sword is always lower than the scale is because punishment can only be dispensed after evidence has been carefully weighed out. The balance (scales) represents weighing out the facts and the evidence to decide a verdict. She symbolizes the fair and equal administration of the law without corruption, greed, prejudice, and favor.

From a spiritual perspective as believers, we must be incredibly mindful that our actions, our efforts, and our decisions are being weighed out daily, spiritually. This raises a concern in me because of the coldness, numbness, and even callousness that is seemingly inundating our nation, where the mindset is if it feels good do it. Don't worry about the consequences or the fall out, because it's your life, and it doesn't matter what anybody thinks. Even though that might be the mindset of the world, it cannot be the mindset of the church.

Th Second Epistle to the Corinthians 6:17 (KJV) states, "Wherefore come out from among them, and be ye separate, saith the Lord, and touch not the unclean thing; and I will receive you." We must understand that the Lord called us to be separated, not segregated! *Separated* means to know our boundaries, but not *segregated*, where we come across as better. The question that we must ask ourselves is this: "If we were put on trial for our Christianity, our faithfulness, and our spiritual separation from the world, and our dedication to God, would there be enough evidence on the scale of decision to convict us?" You see, profession is one thing, but possession is truly another. The spiritual scales reveal and represent so many things. For instance, what is the most important, what is the most significant, and what matters the most.

In November of 2023, our church took a team to Washington, DC, to minister at David's Tent. David's Tent began in 2015 on the

National Mall in Washington, DC. It is a 1,600-square-foot tent where, seven days a week, twenty-four hours a day, there is continual worship and prayer at this nondenominational venue. We took almost one hundred people with us that consisted of our band and praise team, our expressive worship team, and others who came to support and be a part of this special time at our nation's capital. Some of our people drove hauling the instruments and the necessary things we needed for ministry, but most of us flew by plane.

About twenty-five of us flew out of the McGhee Tyson Airport located in Knoxville, Tennessee. Several of the twenty-five who flew with my wife and I had never flown in an airplane before. Nerves were about to get the best of some of them, yet to the others their excitement brought simple joy. As we were on board the plane with an aisle seat, I held the hand of one of our young girls who intentionally sat by me because her nerves were about to get the best of her. Sitting next to her with a window view was another young girl. She was one of our members who had never flown before, so she was excited and enthused. Every little nuance was a big deal to her, from the plane taking off to its gradual climb to the eventual height needed.

She looked out her window, and with every dip and turn of the plane, she carefully pointed seemingly at everything, from how small things looked to the clouds we were flying in and then eventually over. In fact, I believe her repeated words were "This is so cool!" So while I was comforting and reassuring the one next to me whose nerves were about to get the best of her, I was also excited for the other one who was totally enjoying her first flying experience on an airplane. In fact, her joy and enthusiasm were inspiring, and she embraced this brand-new experience. She was so happy, and she organically expressed and showed it. Her simplistic excitement was contagious.

Even though I have personally flown many times both national and international, her excitement and joy affected me and those around her. Her simple reaction and careful attention to detail breathed a breath of fresh and pure joy. All the while, the one next to her who had been a bundle of nerves was now starting to calm down.

The pure joy that this young lady displayed brought in many ways stability to concern and peace in a time of worry. In fact, her joy brought order to chaos! This is one of the many reasons why pure joy is so important. When someone is unsettled, the pure joy of a believer can bring some peace and tranquility to someone struggling. If there is anything that our country needs, it is for the people of God to become baptized in fresh joy. A joy that cannot be explained, but one that can be on display for the world to see and know that there is true joy that can bring balance, hope, and peace.

By nature, I have a very serious side where I take everything in and process it to attempt to come to a proper conclusion. Then there is a side of me that might pull a prank or share a funny video. I understand that balance is essential because not all things are serious, and neither are all things funny. Simply put, it's just understanding how to balance a life of true joy in the Lord. True joy is not when everything is going your way. True Joy is knowing the promises of God and then applying them to your everyday life. One of my favorite passages of scripture to read is in Acts, the eighth chapter. The backdrop of this passage is that at a time of great persecution by Saul who would eventually be converted, and his name would become Paul. He was arresting believers for their faith and was arresting and persecuting them. And at this time of great attack and affliction, a revival broke out in Samaria.

People were saved, healed, and delivered from demonic spirits as the Word was being preached, proclaimed, and prophesied. The Bible said in Acts 8:8, "And there was great joy in that city." The word *joy* in this instance means so many wonderful things such as cheerfulness, calm delight, gladness, and exceeding joy. True joy brings so much balance to our life. Because there are times when we need cheerfulness, calm delight, gladness, and exceeding joy to deal with and even counter the chaos that is in the world.

I pray that while you are reading this, you are determining in your mind that you are going to deliberately discipline yourself, your heart, and your mind to live, walk, and operate in a balance of joy. Friend, our time on this planet is truly too short to allow the cares of life to steal the true joy that the Lord wants every one of us to experience every day of our life. Acts 17:28 (KJV), For in Him we live, and move and have our being. Truly, everything evolves, involves, and revolves around our relationship with the Lord Jesus. Because in Him, we are continually evolving and everything must involve him and through him we are all perpetually revolving. Continually evolving means to be developing gradually, especially from the simple to the more complex.

Involving means to include what is necessary to achieve what is desired. *Perpetually revolving* means to become concerned, absorbed, consecrating, and focusing. Our lives are an open book to be read by all men. If someone is reading your life, what conclusion would they come to? This is truly a fair question because we all live according to our own personal revelation and realization that we have obtained and accrued through our personal devotion time, as well as what we have heard and received. The only conclusion is that true joy is only found in the Lord Jesus Christ. Counting it all joy simply means whatever happens in my life, I know Jesus has me. Counting it all joy simply means I have truly found the answer, and it is Christ in me, the hope of glory (Colossians 1:17).

May we all, as Christians of whatever denomination, preference that we have chosen to pursue and be filled with the joy of the Lord and be a consistent example and faithful witness of Jesus Christ. In 1 Timothy 4:12 (NET), "Let no one look down on you because you are young but set an example for the believers in your speech, conduct, love, faithfulness, and purity." The apostle Paul reveals five ways that all believers are to be examples in speech or how we express our faith:

> *In speech*, or how we express our faith.
> *In conduct*, or in the manner we behave in public
> that reveals our faith.
> *In love*, or with deep affection that displays our
> faith.
> *In faithfulness* that shows the stability of our faith.
> *In purity* that reveals the sincerity of our faith.

In closing, I pray that as you have read this book, studied the Scripture references, and allowed the Holy Spirit to speak to you, you have come to the conclusion that in life, whether in blessing or even in frustration, we can walk in balance, love, and maturity. We can truly count it all joy because we have the revelation that joy is not just the natural things that we have obtained, but that real joy is in a dedicated, devoted life to the Lord Jesus.

ABOUT THE AUTHOR

It was at the beginning of my second semester of college, around 1980, that I felt a tug at my heart by the Holy Spirit. Shortly thereafter, I gave my heart to the Lord. I was truly and radically saved. Everything changed for me in that moment. Old things were passed away, and behold all things became new, just like 2 Corinthians 5:17 said it would be.

On April 16, 1983, I married my wife, Kim, after only six months of courtship. Although a short dating period, we both knew we wanted to spend the rest of our lives together. In 1987, two of the most important things happened in my life: May 10, our daughter, Savanna, was born; and in September of that year, I accepted my call into ministry. Needless to say, our lives were never the same again.

Ministry and parenting brought us so much joy and fulfillment. Yes, there were challenges and tests that shook us, but God was faithful through it all. To this day, He is still showing Himself faithful. We evangelized and did our best to help as many churches as we could.

From 1990 to roughly 1993, we were associate pastors at Morgan Branch Pentecostal Church in Manchester, Kentucky, and the congregation was certainly loved by us. In 1994, we were contacted by East Pittsburg Pentecostal Church, which at that time was without a pastor, to come and minister. We continued for several weeks after that until I was elected as full-time pastor on October 21, 1994.

About a year and a half in, the wind of the Holy Spirit began to blow, and we started experiencing growth. Soon thereafter, we were in need of a bigger facility. In November of 2001, we moved into our new facility. In 2007, we felt prompted to change the church name to Freedom Christian Fellowship. Nearly after thirty years of pastoring at Freedom, we are still seeing growth and even looking to expand once again. To God be the glory!